OUR
ANCESTRY

OUR ANCESTRY

ROBERT WYETH

To order additional copies of this book, contact:
Xlibris
UK TFN: 0800 0148620 (Toll Free inside the UK)
UK Local: 02036 956328 (+44 20 3695 6328 from outside the UK)
www.Xlibrispublishing.co.uk
Orders@Xlibrispublishing.co.uk
827256

CONTENTS

Section 4: Going Back

Section 5: A Timelines

ACKNOWLEDGEMENTS

The ancestors provide the framework by which the
ethical and religious purity of us can be maintained.

They form a continuous line of humanity
from the past, to us in the present.

Whether we approve or disapprove of their actions
but we don't know what the circumstances
of their lives are, or what
things might happen to them.

PREFACE

My manuscript needs to be updated because the work I have done with our grandparents, some dates have altered, I have corrected the events with help of my relatives.

When a person was born and when they are died in the same place, it was noted as 'there at'.

I have updated our DNA, but the process was updated and amended at the laboratories in America for our father and mother.

I have added Nicholas in 1510 to the 'Westwood' family.

Familes under the 'Comport'. Following on from Emily Isobella Comport.

Families under the 'Plantagenet', including Edward I, Henry III and John Kings of England.

Families under the 'Wyeth'. Following on from George Wythe.

Most of the children who are registered with their birth dates, where possible. This is the way to see how the family were joined together. Redefining most of our families with the children. I have underlined the children, as you can see.

I have collected together a lot of documents where families are present, so if there are any doubts, just come back to me.

SUMMARY

Each of us can trace our family going back many years such that many of us have relatives going back into the eighth century. However, we may not find a relative in most official records. Why not?

The official records go back to 1500 AD. Before that, there were written records only of those who were rich. There were no other written records at all: no censuses, no birth certificates, no marriage documents, no death testimonials, nothing. All records were on scraps of paper; many cannot be understood at all, and even if you can read the script, the writing is terrible and unreadable. Most people were not listed at all.

Many rich families had scribes who could record them; others are mentioned in poetry or listed in books. For this reason, my family record goes back a long way, I have discovered a Lady Alice Gage in my ancestry. This is good news as it makes a lot of difference to exploring my family's past. It doesn't mean that I am better than you, only that my descendants contains a rich woman. Don't worry, your records go back a long way too, even more so than mine.

I have traced my ancestors and those of my wife and I have included our mothers. Many names are new, and you may therefore be surprised at what I have discovered in the past.

All individuals have been listed by the male surname, because that is what the chronological record is all about. Many worthwhile people have contributed their effort, adding information as they have found it. It has been a gradual process involving many people trying to trace their own ancestors.

Uncertainty remains over many dates and places in my records. My list was compiled on a computer using the websites www.ancestry.co.uk, www.myheritage.com and www.wikipedia.org. I have also a number of records from the relatives.

If any dates are incorrect or I have missed a person out the fault is mine, not anyone else.

SECTION 1: THE PAST

ROMANS

In BC 55 Britain was invaded by Julius Caesar, the governor of France. By Caesar's time, Rome controlled an empire that stretched from Spain to the New East.

The Romans had grand buildings constructed of marble, while Britain was a country of mud huts, without any towns. The Romans were interested in art, philosophy and history, while the British could neither read nor write. They were not savages in some ways Celtic art was superior to that of the Romans, but the Romans thought of the British as barbarians.

The British were led by Cassivellaunus and had chariots but they could not stop the Romans. From the time of the invasion. Britain enjoyed the benefits of trade with the great Roman Empire. Roman merchants came to Britain, and the Roman influence was strong and lasting.

In 43 AD the Romans landed in Kent. Although they were chiefly interested in the fertile south east, they soon discovered that lead and copper lay further west in the hills.

In 61 AD a dramatic revolt broke out, and the Roman soldiers behaved badly towards the local people. They raped the king's daughters and gave their mother, Queen Boudicca, a whipping. A wild army swept upon Colchester, London and St Albans and killed the Roman soldiers.

In 120 AD the Emperor Hadrian marked the frontier between England and Scotland with a great wall between Newcastle and Carlisle. Later, in 142 AD another wall was built further north. Serious outbreaks came from Scotland.

By the third century, there was no mistaking the decadence of Rome. Ordinary people seemed to care for nothing and the aristocracy were weak. Standards of education had fallen, inflation was leading Britain into ruin. Written records disappeared before 400 AD and coins and pottery became scarce.

ANGLO-SAXONS

The three largest Anglo-Saxon tribes apparently from Germany came over to Britain, but there is no actual evidence of this: no archaeological digs and not even a trace of where they might have been. It is possible that the Saxons gained an advantage over the Romans, who vanished from Britain in 406 AD.

From the Anglo-Saxon tribes, simple tribal chiefs who were successful in war became kings. The king was elected, he did not gain his crown by right of inheritance.

The Anglo-Saxons were less worried by money problems after the departure of the Roman forces. In return for the support of his subjects, the Anglo-Saxon king gave them protection and rewarded them with grants of land. Trade led to the availability of goods like salt, fish and metals.

The nobleman lived in a windowless, barn-like hall, built of wood, which was surrounded by smaller houses and protected by a stockade. Stone buildings appeared in the ninth century. Furniture was simple, consisting of trestle tables, benches, and straw mattresses on the floor.

Most of northern Europe was converted to Christianity by missionaries and Christianity was a great calming influence. To begin with, it introduced more education; most books were written in Latin.

Before the eighth century the British Isles were raided by another non-Christian people, from Scandinavia called the Vikings. These sea-going people dominated half the land between Scotland and England.

RURAL LIFE

In the Middle Ages most people lived in rural, village communities. Towns were rare and country life followed a regular pattern each year. In spring, fields were ploughed, crops were sown and sheep were sheared. In summer crops were tended and hay was made. Each village was more or less self-sufficient with its own blacksmith, craftsman and church.

From daily life:

- A thatcher was a craftsman who made watertight roofs from bundles of dried reeds.
- A medieval plough turned the soil to make fields ready for crops to be planted.
- A scythe was razor sharp. Sickles and scythes were used for cutting crops.
- The grain was separated from the husk by threshing or beating with a heavy flail.
- The local landowner lived in a large house, the manor house and his peasants provided food for his household.

In forested regions with plenty of lumber, houses were built with wooden frames and thatched roofs. The walls were made from wattle and daub; woven strips of wood covered by a mixture of clay and straw.

Thorny forests, barren heaths, swamps and marshes covered much of the land. Rivers were not neatly confined to their banks but spread over the fields. Bears, wolves and wild boar roamed the forests and there were vast numbers of trees.

Most people spent their whole lives in the countryside, separated from each other by forests, woods or animals. They were content to let the world go by. This is what it was like during the 'Dark Ages'.

HERALDRY

There are certain members of the population who have official precedence and are permitted the use of armorial bearings. Historically these people made proclamations, carried official messages and oversaw tournaments. The presence of such a person can be viewed as a sign that something is about to happen.

However, when a person carries a heraldic sign, they are making a prediction or intending to indicate an official position. Historic records may indicate that they held an important position.

The area of chivalric titles is one into which I haven't ventured into. While my own information is very limited, there are several books indicating the reasons for and types of heraldry. Heraldry is something that may take you further back into the past; you may, or may choose not to pursue it.

There are several indications of heraldry back early than 1600 AD

CHIVALRIC TITLES

Many titles are held in Britain, but others are held in other countries of the England, including Wales, Scotland, France and even Israel.

What follows is a brief list of chivalric titles. You can see the differences between them: a king exerts more authority than a duke; the same is true of a baron as compared to a knight.

For example:

- Emperor / Empress
- King / Queen
- Prince / Princess
- Duke / Duchess
- Count / Countess
- Earl
- Viscount / Viscountess
- Baron / Baroness
- Knight
- Lord / Lady

In Europe in the Early Middle Ages, knighthood was conferred upon mounted warriors. During the High Middle Ages, knighthood was considered a lower class of nobility.

By the Late Middle Ages, the rank had become associated with the ideals of chivalry, a code of conduct for the perfect, courteous

Christian warrior. Often, a knight was a vassal who served as an elite fighter, a bodyguard or a mercenary for a lord, receiving payment in the form of land holdings. The kings trusted the knights, who were skilled in battle on horseback. Knighthood in the Middle Ages was closely linked with horsemanship.

In the Late Middle Ages, as gunpowder took the place of swords and lances, new methods of warfare began to render classical knights in armour obsolete, although the title remained in many countries. Today, however, the knight has ceased to exist.

ENGLISH RULERS

The list below details the monarchs of England from William the Conqueror to the end of the reign of the Tudors. This shows you what line of kings the knights had to serve in the Early, Middle and Late Middle Ages.

The list below gives you some idea when they reined not the dates where they lived (in AD).

Normans

1066–1087	William I (William the Conqueror)
1087–1100	William II
1100–1135	Henry I
1135–1154	Stephen

Plantagenets

1154–1189	Henry II
1189–1199	Richard I
1199–1216	John
1216–1272	Henry III
1272–1307	Edward I
1307–1327	Edward II
1327–1377	Edward III
1377–1399	Richard II

Lancasters

1399–1413	Henry IV
1415–1422	Henry V
1422–1461	Henry VI

Yorks

1461–1483	Edward IV
1483	Edward V
1483–1485	Richard III

Tudors

1485–1509	Henry VII
1509–1547	Henry VIII
1547–1553	Edward VI
1553–1558	Mary I
1558–1605	Elizabeth I

EUROPE'S TIMELINE

Looking back you can see what the situation was like in Europe (in AD).

476	The last Western Roman Emperor is disposed.
800	Charlemagne is allowed to be Roman Emperor by the Pope.
889	The Frankish Empire breaks up into France, Germany and Italy.
900	Waves of migrants from Central Asia reach Eastern Europe.
950	The first stone castles are built in Europe.
988	Vladimir, Grand Prince of Kiev, converts to Christianity.
1030	The Normans conquer southern Italy and Sicily.
1066	William of Normandy invades England to claim the throne.
1096	The First Crusade against the Holy Land begins.
1202	The Fourth Crusade sacks Constantinople.
1209	Saint Francis founds the Franciscan Order.
1215	King John seals the Magna Carta.
1237	The Mongols invade Russia and Eastern Europe under Genghis Khan.
1327	The earliest evidence of the use of gunpowder in weapons.

1337	The Hundred Years' War between England and France begins.
1347	The Black Plague reaches Europe.
1381	The Peasants' Revolt occurs in England.
1415	The English defeat the French in the Battle of Agincourt.
1419	The Siege of Orleans is lifted by Joan of Arc's forces.
1450	Johannes Gutenberg produces the first printed books in Europe.
1517	The Protestant Reformation commences.
1520	The reign of Suleiman I over the Ottoman Empire begins.
1572	St Bartholomew's Day Massacre of protestants occurs in France.
1588	The English fleet defeat the Spanish Armada.
1599	The Edict of Nantes: France gives Catholics and Huguenots equal rights.
1603	King James VI unites England and Scotland.
1610	King Henry IV of France is assassinated.
1618	The Thirty Years' War in Europe begins.
1642	The English Civil War ends with the execution of King Charles I.
1665	The Black Plague arrives in England.
1666	The Great Fire of London occurs.
1789	The French revolution gets underway with the storming of the Bastille.
1800	The Union of Britain and Ireland occurs.

DNA TESTS

The DNA results for myself and my wife our ethnicity estimates are as follows:

Robert: (according to Ancestry.co.uk)

78%	England and North-western Europe.
11%	Scotland.
5%	Wales
3%	Ireland.
2%	Germanic Europe.
1%	Basque.

(according to MyHeritage.com)

94.6%	England.
4.3%	Ireland, Scotland and Wales.
1.1%	Eastern Europe.

Carol:

88%	England and North-western Europe.
7%	Scotland.
4%	Germanic Europe
1%	Norway

England and North-western Europe

The history of Britain, the heart of our England & North-western Europe region is often presented as one group of invaders after another displacing the native population. The Romans, Anglo-Saxons, Vikings, and Normans all left their mark on Britain both politically and culturally. However, the story of Britain is far more complex. In fact, modern studies suggest the earliest populations weren't wiped out, but adapted and absorbed the new arrivals.

1 - Prehistoric Britain

Sea levels were still low enough for Stone Age hunter-gatherers to cross from mainland Europe to Britain on foot. Farming spread to the islands and the inhabitants built their remarkable and puzzling stone monuments, including Stonehenge.

Beginning in about BC 2500, successive waves of tribes settled in the region. These tribes are often called Celts. The Celts were not a nation in any sense, but a widespread group of tribes that shared a common cultural and linguistic background. Originating in central Europe, they spread through most of western Europe, the British Isles, and the Iberian Peninsula. Their dominance could not withstand the rise of the Roman Empire.

After defeating the Celts of Gaul (modern-day France and surrounding areas), the Romans invaded the British Isles in 43 AD. Most of southern Britain was conquered and occupied over the course of a few decades and became the Roman province of Britannia. Hadrian's Wall in the north of England, marked the approximate extent of Roman control. The Roman presence largely wiped out most traces of earlier cultures in England even replacing the language with Latin.

2 - Germanic Tribes Invade

With the decline of its Western Empire, Rome largely withdrew from Britannia in 410 AD. As the Romans left, tribes from northern Germany and Denmark stepped in. The Germanic Angles and Saxons soon controlled much of the territory that had been under Roman rule, while the Jutes from Denmark occupied some smaller areas in the south. The new settlers imposed their language and customs on the local inhabitants in much the same way that the Romans had. The Germanic language spoken by the Angles would eventually develop into English.

3 - Viking Invasions and the Danelaw

During the 8th century, seafaring Scandinavians began raiding coastal areas in Europe. Known as the Vikings, they were not just warriors and pillagers. They also established numerous trade ports and settlements throughout the Western world, including the British Isles, Russia, Iceland, and the Iberian Peninsula. A group of Vikings that settled in northern France became known as the Normans. By the early 11th century, ruled a great and powerful region, sanctioned by the French crown.

4 -The Danelaw

Danish Vikings began to invade northern and eastern England in 876 AD and eventually came to control a third of the country, defeating several smaller Anglo-Saxon kingdoms. The rulers of the Danelaw, as the Viking area became known, struggled for nearly 80 years with the remaining English kings over the region. The balance of power swung back and forth, with an English king, Edward the Elder, gaining the upper hand in the early 900 AD and a Danish king, Cnut the Great, ruling England, Norway and Denmark from 1016 to 1035 AD. After the deaths of Cnut's sons, the throne returned to Anglo-Saxon control, but their rule was short-lived. The Normans of France led by William the Conqueror, sailed across the English Channel and claimed the throne of England, defeating Harold Godwinson at the Battle of Hastings in 1066 AD.

5 - The Houses of Plantagenet & Tudor

The Norman kings, ruling primarily from France, gave rise to the House of Plantagenet, a line of kings that began to consolidate and modernise the kingdom of England. Beginning in 1277 AD, Edward I put down a revolt in Wales and led a full-scale invasion, bringing Wales under control of the English crown. He then seized political control of Scotland during a succession dispute, leading to a rebellion there. Edward's campaign against the Scots wasn't entirely successful and remained unresolved at his death. By decisively defeating Edward's son at Bannockburn in 1314 AD, the Scots assured their independence. The House of Plantagenet continued to reign until the 15th century. Towards the latter half of the 15th century the houses of York and the Lancaster, the most powerful Plantagenet branches, fought a series of wars for control of the throne. Those wars ended with the Battle of Bosworth Field on 22 August 1486. At Bosworth Field Henry Tudor defeated Richard III. Henry took the throne as Henry VII and ushered in the reign of the House of Tudor. The reign of the Tudors lasted from Henry VII through Elizabeth I in 1603 AD.

6 - The British Empire

After the defeat of the Spanish Armada in 1588 AD, England established itself as a major naval power. As European nations began founding colonies around the world, England was well positioned to compete for territories of its own. Religious and political upheavals in England in the 17th and 18th centuries played critical roles in early American history, as dissidents left England seeking religious freedom. Later emigrations from England to the Americas ensured a powerful English influence on American culture and society.

The loss of its thirteen American colonies in 1783 AD is seen as a transition point from the First British Empire to the Second British

Empire. In the Americas Britain shifted its attention north to Canada, where many Loyalists migrated after America won its independence. To make up for lost wealth in America, Britain also paid greater attention to Asia, the Pacific, and later Africa. In the 1770 AD James Cook travelled along eastern Australia and New Zealand, claiming them for Great Britain. Britain set up penal colonies in Australia, and over 80 years transported more than 165,000 convicts to Australia. Through the East India Company the British Empire gained more control in Asia. Throughout the early 19th century the East India Company gained control over Java, Singapore, Hong Kong, and India. The Government of India Act in 1858 AD established the British Raj, with Queen Victoria as Empress of India, and India became one of the British Empire's most important colonies. By the end of the 19th century it was said that the sun never set on the British Empire because its colonies stretched around the world.

SECTION 2: WYETH

Old English pre-7th century 'withthe' or the middle English 'wythe' meaning willow tree, and would have referred to someone who lived by a willow tree.

A coat of arms granted to the Wythe family depicts three gold griffins walking in a red shield.

WYETH

Robert Malcolm Wyeth married Carol Jean Spink at Hornchurch, Essex in 1979.

Robert was mechanical engineering and had been a project engineer involving in heavy lifting projects and finally, a paper mill. He had written several computer programs, including stock calculation and the contractor induction programs.

Children are Josephine, Miranda.

He was born in 1952.

Malcolm George Ralph Wyeth married Dorothy Isobel Fisher at Chelmsford, Essex in 1949.

Children are Philip 1950, Robert 1952 and Linda 1955.

Malcolm was called up for the second world war (1939–1945) and served in North India. Afterwards, he didn't return to university, where he had been studying physics, but instead worked in accountancy. He worked in London for a university, where he was head of the department of accountancy.

He was born in 1919 at West Ham, Essex and died in 2003 at Hornchurch, Essex, aged 84.

George William Wyeth married his second wife, Margurrite Louise King at West Ham, Essex in 1917.

George worked as a chemist.

Children are Olive, Ethel Constance 1900, Mabel Inez 1908., Malcolm George Ralph 1919, Bernard Allan Champness 1923 and Jean 1925.

He was born in 1875 at Pimlico, Middlesex and died in 1955 at Lewisham, London, aged 80.
She was born in 1883 at Thurlow, Suffolk and died in 1960 at Sidcup, London, aged 77.

George Champness Wyeth married his first wife Martha Louisa French at St Nicholas church in Brighton, Sussex in 1869.

Children are George William 1870, Edith Elizabeth 1877, Edith Emma 1878, Alice Emma 1879, Charles Ernest 1880, Henry James 1882, Alfred Champness 1884, Annie Eliza 1885, Louise Maud 1886, Charlotte Amy 1892.

He was born in 1848 at Pimlico, Middlesex and died in 1927 at Richmond, Surrey, aged 79.
She was born in 1848 at Edmonton, Middlesex and died in 1930, aged 82.

William Henry Wyeth married his second wife Millicent Wyeth at London in 1837.

Children are Henry D 1834, David 1841, Eliza Henrietta 1843, Elizabeth Ann 1846, George Champness 1848, Sarah Ann 1851.

He was born in 1810 at Reigate, Surrey and died in 1871 at Lambeth, London, aged 61.
She was born in 1808 at Bishops Stortford and died in 1881 at Lambeth, London, aged 73.

William Wyeth married Martha Selway in 1804.

Children are <u>William Henry</u> 1810, Charles James 1714.

He was born in 1783 at Sherbourne St John, Basingstoke and died in 1843 at Marylebone, London, aged 60.
She was born in 1783 and died in 1837, aged 54.

Charles Wyath married Sarah Rampton at Sherborne St John, Hampshire in 1773.

Children are Sarah 1774, James 1775, Charles 1776, <u>William</u> 1783.

He was born in 1744 at Hartley Wespall, Hampshire, and died in 1831 at Sherborne St John, Hampshire, aged 87.
She was born in 1745 at Hampshire and died in 1789 at Sherborne St John, Hampshire, aged 44.

Abraham Wyeth married Elizabeth Humber at Sherborne St John, Hampshire in 1737.

Children are Elisabeth 1738, Sarah 1739, Abraham 1742, <u>Charles</u> 1744.

He was born in 1721 at Heckfield, Hampshire and died in 1781 at All Hallows, London, aged 60.
She was born at Hampshire and died at Whitechapel, Middlesex, in 1807.

George Wythe married Barbara Nash in 1718.

Children are George, <u>Abraham</u> 1721, Mark 1722, Jonathan 1725, Catherine 1729, John 1731.

He was born in 1680 at Odiham, Hampshire and died in 1740 at Hazeley or Heckfield, Hampshire, aged 60.
She was born in 1692 at Odiham, Hampshire and died in 1752 at Hazeley or Heckfield, Hampshire, aged 60.

Thomas Withe married Mary Wythe.

Children are Mary 1637, Anne 1647.

He was born in 1620 and died in 1690 there at Framlingham, Suffolk, aged 70.
She was born in 1620 and died in 1685, aged 65.

Richard Wythe married Joane Wythe.

Children are Thomas 1620, Elizabeth 1627, Joane 1636, Edmund 1640, Katharine 1643.

She was born in 1605 and died in 1685, aged 80.

John Wythe married Emma Elizabeth Jannings in 1573.

Children are Jonathan, George 1577, Dorothy 583, Thomas 1586, Daniel 1589, Agnes 1590, Humphrey 1591, Eleanor 1593, Laurence 1584, Jane 1590, Richard 1596, Rose 1599, Nicholas 1600.

He was born in 1561 and died in 1605 there at Saxtead, Suffolk, aged 44.
She was born in 1568 and died in 1602, aged 34.

Thomas Wise married his first wife Alice de Girling in 1559.

Children are John 1561, Francis 1562, Robert 1563, Thomas 1563, Benjamin 1565, John 1565, Margaret Elizabeth 1565.

He was born in 1532 and died in 1593 there at Tilshead, Wiltshire, aged 61.
She was born in 1544 and died in 1640, aged 96.

John Wyse married Margaret Willington in 1531.

Children are Hen, John William, John, Thomas 1532.

He was born in 1505 and died in 1544 there at Saxtead, Suffolk, aged 39.

She was born in 1505 and died in 1561, aged 56.

Oliver Wyse married Margaret Elizabeth Tremayne.

He was born in 1465 and died in 1505, aged 40.

She was born in 1436 and died in 1526, aged 90.

FISHER

Dorothy Isobel Fisher

Dorothy was a midwife at Chelmsford Hospital before she married Malcolm.

She was born in 1918 at Chelmsford, Essex, and died in 2012 at Hornchurch, Essex, aged 94.

Frederick Charles Fisher married Lucretia Dolly Wyard at Croydon, Surrey in 1918.

Children are <u>Dorothy Isobel</u> 1918, Jean, Richard, Elizabeth.

Richard was a good driver in a Sherman tank but he caught fire when a Tiger tank opened fire and he was badly burnt. He went into hospital and outlived the second world war.

Frederick had worked as a builder but received a leg wound in the First World War (1914–1918). He worked as a caterer, delivering food and other supplies to the front during the war.

He was born in 1892 and died in 1972 at Chelmsford, Essex, aged 80.

James John Fisher Hardingham married Emily Isobella Comport at Bermondsey, Surrey in 1880.

Children are Emily Ethel 1881, Alice Maud 1884, Florence Beatrice 1885, James John 1883, Herbert Ralph 1890, <u>Frederick Charles</u> 1892 and Isabella 1893.

James was a card trimmer. He was convicted of a crime in 1877 and sent to Wormwood Scrubs for seven years but he was released after one year.

He was born at 1845 at Guestwick, Norfolk and died in 1894 at Aylmerton, Norfolk, aged 49.
She was born in 1858 at Bermondsey, Suffolk and died in 1907 at Middlesex, aged 49.

Matthew Fisher married Mary Hardingham at Reepham, Norfolk in 1820.

Children are <u>John</u> 1845, William 1848, Matthew 1849, Robert 1852.

He was born in 1814 and died in 1859 at Reepham, Norfolk, aged 45.
She was born in 1820 and died in 1852 at Reepham, Norfolk, aged 32.

John Fisher married Jane Parratt in 1785.

Children are Matthew 1786, Jane 1789, Mathew 1791, Richard 1795, John 1799, Thomas 1801, James 1802, Susannah 1805, Mary 1808.

He was born in 1760 at Bardney, Lincolnshire and died in 1853 at Market Rasen, Lincolnshire, aged 93.
She was born in 1767 and died in 1835, aged 68.

Matthew Fisher married Susanna Rushton in 1760.

Child is <u>John</u> 1760.

He was born in 1736 at Linwood, Lincolnshire and died in 1814 at Teably, Lincolnshire, aged 78.
She was born in 1736 and died in 1763 at Bardney, Lincolnshire, aged 27.

John Fisher married Mary Wright at Lindwood, Lincolnshire in 1726.

Children are John 1730, <u>Matthew</u> 1736, Elizabeth 1738, Catherine 1740, Richard 1742

He was born in 1699 at Apley, Lincolnshire and died in 1746 at Linwood, Lincolnshire, aged 49.

William Fisher married Elizabeth Bean at St Martin, Lincolnshire in 1698.

Child is <u>John</u> 1699

He was born in 1672 and died in 1750 at Apley, Lincolnshire, aged 78.
She was born in 1675 at Timberland, Lincolnshire.

Christopher Fisher married his first wife Elizabeth Williams.

Children are Alice 1654, William 1659, Christopher 1662, Thomas 1666, <u>William</u> 1672, William 1715.

He was born in 1641.

COMPORT

Emily Isobella Comport

She was born in 1854 in Bermondsey, Surrey and died at 1946 in Middlesex, aged 88.

Charles Comport married Mary Ann Roper at Dartford, Kent in 1840.

Children are Charles Augustus 1841, Mary Ann 1846, Ebenezer J 1848, Augusta M E 1849, Richard R 1852, Emily Isabella 1854, William 1856, Alice 1859.

He was born in 1820 at Southhampton, Hampshire and died in 1888 at London, aged 68.
She was born in 1821 at Rotherhithe, Surrey and died in 1851, aged 30.

Ebenezer Comport married his first wife Elizabeth.

Children are Charles 1820, George 1831, Ebenezer 1806, Joseph 1812, Henry 1813, Ann 1814, Samuel 1816, Charles 1818, Maria 1819, John 1821, Susanna 1823, Joseph.

He was born in 1784 at Shoreditch, Middlesex and died in 1856 at Andover, Hampshire, aged 72.
She was born in 1791 at Andover, Hampshire.

Joseph Comport married Susanna French at Westminster, London in 1776.

Children are Ebenezer 1776, Anna 1778, Mary Ann 1781, <u>Ebenezer</u> 1784, Anna Elizabeth 1792.

He was born in 1737 at France and died in 1808 at Clerkenwell, Middlesex, aged 71.
She was born in 1754 at Bartholomew, London and died in 1795, aged 41.

Ebenezar Comport married Elizabeth Steely in 1728 at Surrey.

Child is <u>Joseph</u> 1737

He was born in 1704 at Holborn, London and died in 1765, aged 61.

Ebenezer Comport married Mary Stephens at London in 1697.

Children are Ebenezar 1704, Joseph 1708.

He was born in 1675 and died in 1733, aged 58.
She was born in 1672.

Nicholas Comport

Child is <u>Ebenezer</u>.

He died in 1679.

WYARD

Lucretia Dolly Wyard

Lucretia was a midwife.

She was born in 1896 at London and died in 1996 at Chelmsford, aged 100.

Ephraim Wyard married his second wife Susan Mary Caddy at Camden, Kent in 1891.

Children are Albert Edward 1866, Florence Lucy 1869, Frederick John 1872, James 1892, John Ernest 1892, Charles Frederick 1894, Lucretia Dolly 1896, Caroline 'Lily' 1899.

Ephraim was a newsagent.

John Ernest died in the Second World War for his ship HMS Natal caught fire.

He was born in 1839 at Ely, Cambridgeshire and died in 1904 at Croydon, Surrey, aged 46.
She was born in 1858 at Greenwich, Kent and died in 1954 at Croydon, Surrey, aged 96.

Walter Wyard married Susan Cadman at Ely, Cambridgeshire in 1836.

Children are William 1837, <u>Ephraim</u> 1839.

He was born in 1808 at Cambridge, Cambridgeshire and died in 1848 at Ely, Cambridgeshire, aged 40.
She was born in 1814 at Isleham, Cambridgeshire and died in 1853 at Ely, Cambridgeshire, aged 39.

William Wyard married Frances Harnton.

Children are Rebecca Elizabeth, Caroline 1804, <u>Walter</u> 1808

He was born in 1780 at Bradfield, Suffolk.
She was born in 1755 at Suffolk.

Thomas Wyard married Ann Maxim at Bradfield, Suffolk in 1777.

Children are Thomas 1778, <u>William</u> 1780, Mary Ann 1783, Susan 1786.

He was born in 1743 at Great Weinetham, Suffolk and died in 1811 at Chelsfield, Kent, aged 68.
She was born in 1756.

William Wyard married Elizabeth Bruer at Whelnetham, Suffolk in 1737.

Children are Ann 1703, William 1706, Elizabeth 1708, James 1710, <u>Thomas</u> 1743.

He was born in 1706 at Horringer, Suffolk and died in 1781 at Great Welnetham, Suffolk, aged 75.
She was born in 1702 and died in 1772, aged 70.

William Wyard married Ann Westham in 1699.

Children are Ann 1703, <u>William</u> 1706, Elizabeth 1708, James 1710, Thomas 1713.

He was born in 1667 at Horringer, Suffolk and died in 1746 at Great Welnetham, Suffolk, aged 79
She died in 1750.

William Wyard married Hannah Cooper in 1664.

Children are Hannah 1665, William 1667, Frances 1668, Rachel 1671, Elizabeth 1723, James 1675, Thomas 1676.

He was born in 1630 and died in 1694 there at Horringer, Suffolk, aged 64.
She was born in 1645 and died in 1696 there at Horringer, Suffolk, aged 51.

James Wyard married Elizabeth Covell in 1621.

Children are Elizabeth 1622, James 1624, Henry 1627, William 1630, Hester 1633, Thomas 1635.

He was born in 1608 and died in 1653 there at Horringer, Suffolk, aged 45.

William Wyard married Elizabeth James.

Child is James 1593.

He was born in 1557 and died in 1630 there in Horringer, Suffolk, aged 73.
She was born in 1565 and died in 1602 there in Caston, Norfolk, aged 37.

Humfrey Wyard he married the second wife Elizabeth Facebrown in 1563.

Children are Richard 1560, Margaret 1562, Humfrey 1564, William 1567

He was born in 1530 and died in 1597 at Earl Soham, Suffolk, aged 67.
She was born in 1520.

Richard Wyard married Agnes Hawes in 1523.

He was born in 1478 and died in 1560, aged 82.
She was born in 1502 and died in 1564 there at Saxtead, Woodbridge, Suffolk, aged 62.

Randall Wyard married Ann Wyard.

SECTION 3: SPINK

From the Anglo-Saxon culture of Britain. Their names reveals that an early member was a person who because of his physical characteristics was referred to as 'the spink', which literally means 'the finch'.

The surname 'Spink' was first found in Northampton where they held a family seat from very ancient times, some say well before the Norman Conquest.

SPINK

Carol Jean Spink

Carol has worked as an occupational therapist and later a music teacher. She has played the keyboard, piano and organ for her church and other people.

She was born in 1957.

Eric Douglas Spink married Kathleen Irene Maud Rutter at Rainham, Essex in 1953.

Children are Carol 1957, Pauline 1959, David 1964.

Eric was in the Ordinance Corps during the Secord World War and was sent to Mombasa, Kenya. Later he worked as Assistant Director for Bowring's Insurance Ltd.

He was born in 1927 at Rainham, Essex and died in 2017 at Hornchurch, Essex, aged 90.

Frederick William Spink married Ethel Maud Perry at Victoria Park, London in 1921.

Children are Kathleen Joyce 1923, Ronald 1923, Freda Jean 1925, Eric Douglas 1927.

Frederick was a railway signalman.

He was born in 1894 at Rainham, Essex and died in 1960 at Romford, Essex, aged 66.

James William Spink married Emma Elizabeth Rivers at Bethnal Green, London in 1883.

Children are Mary Ann Florence 1884 Walter James 1884, Elizabeth Louisa 1887, Jessie May 1889, Percy Rivers 1892, Frederick William 1894.

James was a cobbler, mending and making shoes.

He was born in 1849 at Saxtead, Suffolk and died in 1939 at Romford, Essex, aged 90.
She was born in 1852 at Bethnal Green, London and died in 1883, aged 31.

William Spink married Mary Ann Rivers in Plomesgate, Suffolk in 1842.

Children are Elizabeth Louise 1844, Amos Rivers 1845, James William 1849, Sarah 1854, Mary Ann 1856.

He was born in 1817 at Saxtead, Suffolk and died in 1902 at Framlingham, Suffolk, aged 85.
She was born in 1819 at Earl Soham, Suffolk and died in 1906 at Framlingham, Suffolk, aged 87.

Issac Spink married Ann Pipe at Plomesgate, Suffolk in 1803.

Children are Isaac 1804, Allen Pipe 1809, John 1813, William 1817, Maria 1821.

He was born in 1781 and died in 1850 at Saxsted, Suffolk, aged 69.
She was born in 1780 at Chediston, Suffolk and died in 1843 at Saxtead, Suffolk, aged 63.

PIPE

Ann Pipe

She was born in 1781 in Chediston, Suffolk and died in 1843 at Saxtead, Suffolk, aged 63.

William Pipe married Hannah Greenard at Chediston, Suffolk in 1774.

Children are Elizabeth 1775, Susan 1775, George 1778, <u>Ann</u> 1783, William 1784, Harriet 1786, Benjamin 1793, James 1793, Greenard 1796.

He was born in 1750 at Framlingham, Suffolk and died in 1827 at Flixton, Suffolk, aged 77.
She was born in 1755 at Chediston, Suffolk and died in 1824 at Framlingham, Suffolk, aged 69.

Edward Pipe married his second wife Elizabeth Stannard at Dennington, Suffolk in 1746.

Children are Ann 1739, Mary 1740, Edward 1742, Samuel 1745, John 1749, <u>William</u> 1750, Elizabeth 1751, Hannah 1754, Susan 1757.

He was born in 1715 at Dennington, Suffolk and died in 1827 at Framlingham, Suffolk, aged 44.

She was born in 1725 at Cratfield, Suffolk and died in 1774 at Framlingham, Suffolk, aged 49.

John Pipe married Mary Ralf at Plomesgate, Suffolk in 1709.

Children are John 1710, James 1712, <u>Edward</u> 1715, James 1715, Mary 1717, William 1721, Samuel 1724, Ralph 1726, Mary 1728, Benjamin 1731, Elizabeth 1732.

He was born in 1674 at Dennington, Suffolk, and died in 1720 at Cransford, Suffolk, aged 73.
She was born in 1688 at Cransford, Suffolk and died in 1735, aged 47.

William Pipe married Anne Girling in 1670.

Children are William 1671, Jeremiah 1674, <u>John</u> 1674, Samuel 1677, Benjamin 1681, James 1683, Anne 1685.

He was born in 1649 at Saxtead, Suffolk, and died in 1731 at Dennington, Suffolk, aged 82.
She was born in 1675 and died in 1746 at Dennington, Suffolk, aged 71.

Wylam Pipe married Sarah Neal in 1634.

Children are Margaret 1637, William 1637, Elizabeth 1641, William 1642, Mary 1643, Sarah Anne 1646, <u>William</u> 1649

He was born in 1611 at Brundish, Suffolk and died in 1650 at Earl Soham, Suffolk, aged 39.
She was born in 1615 and died in 1649 there at Wilby, Suffolk, aged 34.

William Pipe married Rebecca Rebacker in 1611.

Children are Matilda, <u>Wylam</u> 1611, Jeremiah 1612, Edward 1615.

He was born in 1586 and died in 1622 at Brundish, Suffolk, aged 36.
She was born in 1590 and died in 1615 there at Brundish, Suffolk, aged 25.

Jerome Pipe married Margaret Dowsing in 1585.

Children are <u>William</u> 1586, Jeromy 1588, Thomas 1591, Margaret 1593, John 1596, Elizabeth 1601, Anne 1604

He was born in 1563 and died in 1631 there at Brundish, Suffolk, aged 68.
She was born in 1563 and died in 1604, aged 41.

William Pipe (the elder) married Mildred Thymblethorpe in 1550.

Children are Edward 1550, Hughe 1551, Ann 1558, Elizabeth 1560, Richard 1561, Dyonese 1563, <u>Jerome</u> 1563, George.

He was born in 1530 and died in 1580 there at Brundish, Suffolk, aged 50.
She was born in 1530 and died in 1580 there at Brundish, Suffolk, aged 50.

Thomas Pipe married Margaret in 1517.

Children are Agnes 1530, <u>William</u> 1530, Jeffery 1540.

He was born in 1500 and died in 1560 there at Brundish, Suffolk, aged 60.
She was born in 1510 and died in 1510 there at Brundish, Suffolk, aged 61.

William Pipe married Margery.

He was born in 1485 and died in 1517, aged 32.
She was born in 1485 and died in 1517, aged 32.

PERRY

Ethel Maud Perry
Ethel worked as a domestic servant.

She was born in 1897 at Dagenham, Essex and died in 1975 at Rainham, Essex, aged 78.

Henry Percy Perry married Alice Jane Baker at Romford, Essex in 1895.

Children are Edwin, Flo, Florence May 1896, Ethel Maud 1897, Lily May 1900, Fredrick James 1902, Ada May 1906, Harry 1908, William George 1910, Minnie 1913, Alice 1916, Elsie 1918.

He was born in 1874 at Hornchurch, Essex and died in 1942 at Dagenham, Essex, aged 68.
She was born in 1876 and died in 1953 there at Hornchurch, Essex, aged 77.

George Perry married Sarah Elizabeth Poole in Roydon, Essex in 1857.

Children are James 1867, Elizabeth 1872, Henry Percy 1874.

He was born in 1833 at Black Notley and died in 1915 at Romford, Essex, aged 82.

Thomas Perry married his first wife Mary Ann Brewer in 1832.

Children are <u>George</u> 1833 William 1846, Hannah 1847, Henry 1849, Charles 1854, Mary 1855, Sarah 1859.

He was born in 1812 at Stebbing, Essex and died in 1888 at Black Notley, Essex, aged 76.

Thomas Perry married Susannah Chopping in 1790.

Child is Susannah 'Anne' 1803.

He was born in 1770 at Stebbing, Essex.
She was born in 1772 at Stebbing, Essex.

POOLE

Sarah Elizabeth Poole

She was born in 1838 at Writtle, Essex and died in 1924 at Romford, Essex, aged 86.

William Poole married Margaret Harris at Essex in 1838.

Children are Henry 1835, Sarah Elizabeth 1838, William 1841, James 1844, Edward 1849, Herbert 1852.

He was born in 1809 at Writtle, Essex, and died in 1892 at Chelmsford, Essex, aged 83.
She was born in 1804 at Stambridge, Essex and died in 1886 at Chelmsford, Essex, aged 82.

Edward Poole married Hannah Bright at Whittington, Shropshire in 1792.

Child is Elizabeth 1795.

He was born in 1767 at Chelmsford, Essex and died in 1838 at Writtle, Essex, aged 70.
She was born at Writtle, Essex, in 1762 and died at Chelmsford, Essex, in 1848, aged 86.

Edward Poole married his first wife Elizabeth Westwood at Writtle, Essex in 1761.

Children are Hannah 1762, John 1763, Sarah 1766, <u>Edward</u> 1767, William 1771, Thomas 1774.

He was born in 1739 and died in 1832 there at Writtle, Essex, aged 93. She was born at Roxwell, Essex, in 1739 and died at Writtle, Essex, in 1767, aged 28.

John Poole married Hannah Holmstead in 1736.

Children are Sarah 1737, <u>Edward</u> 1739, John 1744.

He was born in 1702 and died there in 1796 at Writtle, Essex, aged 94. She was born in 1715 at Writtle, Essex and died in 1763, aged 48.

William Poole married Mary Herrridge in 1702.

Child is <u>John</u> 1702.

He was born in 1660 at Essex.
She was born in 1660 at Essex.

WESTWOOD

Elizabeth Westwood

She was born in 1739 at Roxwell, Essex and died in 1767 at Writtle, Essex, aged 28.

William John Westwood married his first wife Ann Luck in 1724 at Essex.

Children are William Edward 1725, Ann 1728, Frances 1730, James 1732, Thomas 1738, Elizabeth 1740, <u>Elizabeth</u> 1739, Sarah 1740.

He was born in 1699 and died in 1767 at Roxwell, Essex, aged 68.
She was born in 1697 at Beauchamp Roding, Essex, and died in 1769 at Roxwell, Essex, aged 72.

Thomas William Westwood married Elizabeth Beverley in 1693.

Children are Jane, William, Thomas 1694, John 1697, <u>William John</u> 1699, Elizabeth 1702, Jane 1705, Daniel 1708.

He was born in 1668 at Roxwell, Essex and died in 1725 at Old Swinford, Worcestershire, aged 57.
She was born in 1673 and died in 1769 there at Roxwell, Essex, aged 96.

Thomas Westwood married his first wife Hannah Lewis at Compton, Somerset in 1665.

Child is <u>Thomas William</u> 1668.

He was born in 1645 and died in 1691 there at Good Easter, Essex, aged 46.
She was born in 1645 at Good Easter, Essex.

Henry Westwood - Yeoman married Mary Butcher at Wimbush, Essex in 1645.

Children are <u>Thomas</u> 1645, Henry 1647, Mary 1649, Ann 1657, Mary 1657.

He was born in 1619 at Great Burstead, Essex and died in 1683 at Wimbush, Essex, aged 64.
She was born in 1623 at Waltham Abbey, Essex.

Nicholas Westwood married Katherine Morgan at Saint Cuthbert, Somerset in 1609.

Children are Katherin 1609, Richard 1610, Phillip 1611, John 1612, James 1615, Elizabeth 1616, <u>Henry</u> 1619, Marie 1621.

He was born in 1590 and died in 1678 there at Essex, aged 88.
She was born in 1593 and died in 1634 there at Essex, aged 59.

Nicholas Westwood married Grace Turnish at Chipping Ongar, Essex in 1591.

Child is <u>Nicholas</u> 1590.

He was born in 1565 at Essex.
She was born in 1565 and died in 1630 there at Essex, aged 65.

Nicholas Westwood

Child is <u>Nicholas</u> 1565

He was born in 1510.

RUTTER

Kathleen Irene Maud Rutter

Kathleen worked at Bowring's Insurance Ltd and worked as a comptometer operator.

She was born in 1931.

Percy Pearson Graham Rutter married Mary Maud Adelaide Blunt at Aston, Warwickshire in 1927.

Children are <u>Kathleen I M</u> 1931, Hilary D 1932, Frank Paul Graham 1937.

Percy was a tool maker.

He was born in 1906 at Halstead, Essex and died in 1995 at Miami, Florida, USA, aged 89.

Frank Rutter married Florence Louisa Clark at Hoxne, Suffolk in 1897.

Children are Olive Blanche 1899, William George 1900, Harold Clifford 1902, Mildred Violet 1904, <u>Pearson Graham</u> 1906, Carol Florence 1909, Lucy Louisa 1912.

Frank was working as a miner, he became a baker in either Beccles or Bungay. Later, he had a business in Halstead.

He was born in 1872 at Stradbrook, Suffolk and died in 1949 at Sutton Coldfield, Warwickshire, aged 77.
She was born in 1877 at Horham, Suffolk and died in 1933 at Birmingham, Warwickshire, aged 56.

William Rutter married his second wife Lucy Harriot Moore at Ipswich, Suffolk in 1872.

Children are <u>Frank</u> 1872, Estella 1873, Lillian 1875, Constance 1876, Leonard Vernon 1877, Daisy 1878, Charles Herbert 1880, Cecil Joseph 1883, Gertrude Violet 1883, Hedley 1884, Mary Primrose 1886, Clarence Arthur 1889.

He was born in 1828 at Glemsford, Suffolk and died in 1904 at Stradbroke, Suffolk, aged 76.
She was born in 1843 at Syleham, Suffolk and died in 1924 at Suffolk, aged 81.

Joseph Rutter married Mary Ann Haygreen at Wipstead, Suffolk in 1822.

Children are Alfred 1824, Emma Elizabeth 1826, <u>William</u> 1828, Mary Ann 1831, Joseph 1832, Sarah Anne 1834, John Thomas 1837, Jane 1840, Robert James 1842.

He was born in 1790 at Wickhambrook, Suffolk and died in 1861 at Bury St Edmunds, Suffolk, aged 71.
She was born in 1801 at Wickhambrook, Suffolk and died in 1849 at Thingoe, Suffolk, aged 48.

Joseph Rutter married Prudence Hurrell at Denston, Suffolk in 1783.

Children are Sally 1785, Molly 1788, <u>Joseph</u> 1790, Betsey 1792, Mary 1794, John 1800, William 1800,

He was born in 1753 at Wickhambrook, Suffolk and died there at 1824, aged 71.

She was born in 1755 at Denston, Suffolk and died in 1837 at Wickhambrook, Suffolk, aged 82.

Thomas Rutter married Sarah Richardson.

Children are John 1752, <u>Joseph</u> 1753.

He was born in 1713 at Bury St Edmunds, Suffolk and died in 1778 at Wickhambrook, Suffolk, aged 65.

She was born in 1730 and died in 1781 there at Suffolk, aged 51.

John Rutterforth Rutter married Susannah Boarly.

Child is <u>Thomas</u> 1713.

He was born in 1680 at Tadlow, Cambridgeshire, and died in 1765 at Wickhambrook, Suffolk, aged 85.

She was born in 1690 at Suffolk and died in 1758 at Wickhambrook, Suffolk, aged 68.

Thomas Rutter married his second wife Ann at Tadlow, Cambridgeshire in 1681.

Children are Anne 1741, <u>John</u> 1680, George 1682, Ann 1683, Henry 1685, William 1688, Thomas James 1690, Mary 1692, James 1695.

He was born in 1647 at Arrington, Cambridgeshire and died in 1702 at Tadlow, Cambridgeshire, aged 55.

She was born in 1661 at Wendy, Cambridgeshire and died in 1705 at Tadlow, Cambridgeshire, aged 44.

Thomas Rutterforth married Anne Rutterforth in 1645.

He died in 1699.

She died in 1685.

William Rutterforth

He was born in 1567 and died in 1653, aged 86.

William Rutter

Children are Marye 1565, Willium 1566, Margaret 1570.

BLUNT

Mary Maud Adelaide Blunt
Mary worked as a power press operator.

She was born in 1902 at Rowley Regis, Staffordshire, and died in 1976 at Whittier, Los Angeles, California, USA, aged 73.

William Blunt married Sarah Ann Peacock at Reddal-Hill, Staffordshire in 1890.

Children are Annie Maria 1890, Arthur 1892, Florence 1894, Daniel 1896, Albert Henry 1898, Walter 1900, <u>Mary Maude Adelaide</u> 1902, Eva 1908, Charles 1910.

William worked as a miner.

He was born in 1864 at Rowley Regis, Staffordshire.
She was born in 1868 at Darbys End, Worcestershire and died in 1955 at Dudley, Staffordshire, aged 87.

Daniel Blunt married Johanna Ashman at Stourbridge, Worcestershire in 1862.

Children are <u>William</u> 1864, Albert 1868, Annie Maria 1870, Arthur 1874, Daniel 1876, Joanna 1877, Enoch 1878, Harry 1879, Clara 1882.

He was born in 1838 at Rowley Regis, Staffordshire and died in 1908 at Dudley, Staffordshire, aged 70.
She was born in 1845 at Brierly Hill, Staffordshire and died in 1897 at Dudley, Staffordshire, aged 52.

William Blunt married Eliza Hanslow at Halesowen, Worcestershire in 1834.

Children are <u>Daniel</u> 1838, Sarah Jane 1840, James Shaw 1843, Thomas 1846, Reuben 1849, William 1851, Arthur 1854.

He was born in 1812 at Dudley, Staffordshire and died there in 1891, aged 79.
She was born in 1814 at Rowley, Staffordshire and died in 1880, aged 66.

Thomas Blunt married his first wife Esther Danks at Walsall, Staffordshire in 1812.

Children are <u>William</u> 1812, Elizabeth 1815, Thomas 1815, Ann 1817, Rhoda 1822, Reuben 1825, Selina 1829, Alfred 1835, Hester 1850, Esther M 1851, Joseph Henry 1855.

He was born in 1793 at Rock, Worcestershire and died in 1868 at Dudley, Worcestershire, aged 75.
She was born in 1793 and died in 1844 at Rock, Worcestershire, aged 51.

William Blunt married Prudence Jesson at Sedgley, Staffordshire in 1774.

Children are John William 1778, Benjamin 1780, Sarah 1786, <u>Thomas</u> 1793, George 1796, Sarah 1796.

He was born in 1755 and died in 1796 there at Ribbesford, Worcestershire, aged 41.
She was born in 1758 at Wednesbury, Staffordshire.

George Blunt married Mary Edwards at Kidderminster, Worcestershire in 1749.

Child is <u>William</u> 1755.

He was born in 1739 and died in 1783 at Worcester, Worcestershire, aged 44.
She was born in 1730 at Worcester, Worcestershire.

George Blunt married Ann Reane at Ribbesford, Worcestershire in 1706.

Child is <u>George</u> 1739.

He was born in 1692 at Ribbesford, Worcestershire.
She was born in 1688.

George Blunt married Ann Clarke at Ribbesford, Worcestershire in 1692.

Child is <u>George</u> 1692.

He was born in 1678.

Thomas Blunt

He was born in 1630 and died in 1684, aged 54.

SECTION 4: GOING BACK

We have completed the Wyeth and Spink ancestry, now we will trace the Wyeth's ancestry going back even further.

FRENCH

Martha Louisa French

She was born in 1847 at Little Gonerby, Lincolnshire, and died in 1917 in Southwark, London, aged 80.

William French married Harriet Flexman at Brighton, Sussex in 1842.

Children are Keturah Mary 1843, Jemima Ellen 1845, <u>Martha Louisa</u> 1847, Georgiana Harriett 1849, George Caleb 1852, Elizabeth Ann 1853, Elizabeth Jane 1854, Ellen Esther 1856, Harriett Dorothy 1858, William Henry 1858, James William 1861.

William and his family ran the Derby Arms in Islingword Road during the late 1800s.

He was born in 1816 at Arlington, Sussex and died in 1896 at Brighton, Sussex, aged 80.
She was born in 1816 at Brighton, Sussex, and died in 1871 at Sussex, aged 55.

George French married Jenny Elliot.

Children are <u>William</u> 1818, George 1818.

He was born at 1779 at Salehurst, Sussex and died in 1867 at Ticehurst, Sussex, aged 88.

George French married Mary Cox in 1777.

Children are Sarah 1778, William 1781, George 1784, James 1786, Frank 1789, Henry 1791, Elizabeth 1794, Robert 1796.

He was born in 1751 at Bodiham, Sussex and died in 1831, aged 80. She was born in 1756.

ELLIOT

Jenny Elliot

She was born in 1795 at Berwick, Sussex and died in 1827, aged 32.

Thomas Elliot married his first wife Sarah Burfield in Berwick, Sussex in 1777.

Children are Mary 1778, Sarah 1778, Ann 1780, Thomas 1783, Elizabeth 1785, Willian 1785, Susannah 1791, Charles 1793, Jenny 1795, Catherine 1797, Fanny 1801, Fleming 1801.

He was born in 1744 and died in 1808 in Berwick, Sussex, aged 64.

BURFIELD

Sarah Burfield

She was born in 1756 at Laughton, Sussex and died in 1823 at Meopham, Kent, aged 67.

William Burfield married Ann Bridger in 1740.

Children are Mary 1742, Robert 1744, William 1746, Thomas 1749, Isaac 1752, Samual 1754, <u>Sarah</u> 1756, Ann 1758.

He was born in 1715 and died in 1760 at Laughton, Sussex, aged 45. She was born in 1723 at Rotherfield, Sussex and died in 1770 at Laughton, Sussex, aged 47.

John Burfield married Elizabeth Ellis at Ripe, Sussex in 1714.

Children are John 1714, <u>William</u> 1715, Robert 1716, James 1721, Thomas 1721, Barbara 1723, Samuel 1729.

He was born in 1686 at Thakeham, Sussex and died in 1754 at Ripe, Sussex, aged 68.
She was born in 1688 at Chalvington, Sussex.

Robert Burfield married Mary Streeter at Pulburough, Sussex in 1667.

Children are James, Abraham 1668, Robert 1670, Mary 1677, Elizabeth 1686, John 1686.

He was born in 1660 at Sussex and died 1725 at Steyning, Sussex, aged 65.
She was born in 1646 at Sussex and died in 1704 at Little Hampton, Sussex, aged 58.

Abraham Burfield married Sybil Hale in 1641.

Child is Robert 1660.

He was born in 1615 at Midhurst, Sussex and died in 1684 at Sussex, aged 69.
She was born in 1620 at Sussex and died in 1678 at Stopham, Sussex, aged 58.

Abraham Burfield married Juditha Ford at Midhurst, Sussex in 1610.

Children are John 1610, Elizabeth 1614, Abraham 1615, William John 1616, Marie 1617.

He was born in 1590 at Midhurst, Sussex and died in 1637 at Tillington, Sussex, aged 47.

FORD

Juditha Ford

She was born in 1590 and died in 1640 there at Guildford, Surrey, aged 50.

Richarde Forde married Anne Tyler at Pirbright, St Michael, Surrey in 1578.

Children are Alice 1613, Sara 1562, <u>Juditha</u> 1590.

He was born in 1540 and died in 1596 there at Petworth, Sussex, aged 56.
She was born in 1562 and died in 1626, aged 64.

Richard Forde married Katherine Hide at St Michael Bassishaw, London in 1544.

Children are <u>Richarde</u> 1540, Joan 1542.

He was born in 1530 and died in 1604 there at Petworth, Sussex, aged 74.
She was born in 1520 at Sussex and died in 1611 at Petworth, Sussex, aged 91.

John Aford married Lady Alice Gage at Herstmonceux, Sussex in 1529.

Child is <u>Richard</u> 1530

He was born in 1505 and died in 1545 there at Herstmonceux, Sussex, aged 40.

Herstmonceux Castle: Herstmonceux is a village and civil parish in the Wealden District of East Sussex. Herstmonceux Castle is brick-built and dates from the 15th century. It is one of the oldest significant brick buildings still standing in England.

GAGE

Lady Alice Gage

Alice was born in 1509 and died in 1540 there at Herstmonceux, Sussex, aged 31.

The records contain references to two women called Alice Gage or Alys Gage.

There are differences between them as follows:

- There are difference between their birth dates Alice and Alys.
- Alice Gage married an Aford, and Alys Gage married a Browne.
- Alice had 1 sons and Alys had 7 sons.
- Both Alice and Alys died in 1540.
- But Alice died in Sussex and Alys died in Surrey.

Why did Alice Gage marry a person without rank? Some examples may illustrate this situation:

Sir John found his children annoying.
He was so wrapped up in the king's business.
He didn't really have time to reason with them.
Sir John had in mind a title and property for his children.
Alice fell for a common soldier and married him.
She collected hostility and advice from all her family.

She was in Herstmonceux village, 20 miles away from her home.
She was clearly obstinate and stubborn.
Alice didn't have any property from her father after she got married.
The soldier was killed and she had only one son, Richard.
Richard moved away from Sussex to Surrey.

Which one is correct?

Sir John Gage KG married Philippa de Guildeford in 1501.

Children are Sir Edward, James, Robert, William, Alys, <u>Alice</u>, Ann, Elizabeth, Cicily.

An esquire of the body to both Henry VII and Henry VIII, he held offices in the Pale of Calais, becoming Comptroller in 1524. After receiving a knighthood in 1525, he moved to the post of Vice-Chamberlain of the Household in 1526, leaving court in 1533. He also represented Sussex three times (1529, 1539 and 1542) in the parliaments of Henry VIII.

John remained active after leaving court, in 1537 attending the baptism of Prince Edward and the funeral of Jane Seymour. He returned and saw his appointment as Comptroller of the Household, Constable of the Tower and as a Privy Counsellor. In his role as Constable of the Tower he supervised the arrangements for the execution of Catherine Howard in 1540.

In 1541 he became a Knight of the Garter (KG) and in 1542 he succeeded to the post of Chancellor of the Duchy of Lancaster. In 1544 he undertook an important role supporting the invasion of France, organising transport and supplies for the army and became a knight banneret.

Present at the funeral of Henry VIII, he was appointed one of the executors of the King's will and a member of Edward VI's Regency Council. Differences soon arose between him and The Duke of Somerset, who expelled him from the council and from his posts of Comptroller and Chancellor when he became Lord Protector in 1547.

John re-joined the council, before resigning upon the accession to power of The Earl of Warwick, later Duke of Northumberland. He was suspended as Constable for not supporting Northumberland's attempt to install Lady Jane Grey as Edward's successor.

The accession of Mary I saw his restoration as Constable and appointment as Lord Chamberlain. He bore Mary's train at her coronation and at her marriage to Philip of Spain. As Constable, he guarded Princess Elizabeth in 1555.

He was born in 1479 at Bustow, Surrey, and died in 1556 at Firle Place, Sussex, aged 77.
She was born in 1480 at Oxfordshire and died in 1521, aged 41.

Firle Place: Firle Place is a manor house in Firle, East Sussex. The family of the Viscounts Gage have owned the land at Firle since acquiring it from the Levett family in the 15th century. The manor house was first built in the late 15th century by Sir John Gage, who made Firle Place his principal home. The external cladding of the building is Georgian, with Caen stone used to make it look like a classical French Chateau. The interior of the house, however, is Tudor in style and is built around a central courtyard. The house has an extensive collection of paintings, porcelain and furniture, including works by Gainsborough, Reynolds, Van Dyck, Raphael, Puligo, Zoffany and Teniers.

William Gage married Agnes Bolney.

Child is John 1479.

William was a landowner.

He was born in 1450 and died in 1496, aged 46.
She was born in 1455 and died in 1501, aged 46.

Sir John Gage married Lady Eleanor St Clere.

Children are William, John.

A deed dated 1446 set out the agreed partition of Sir Thomas St Clere lands between his three daughters (and their husbands).

The agreement involved John and Eleanor receiving the following share:

- In Sussex: The manors of Heighton St Clere, Hoathly and Tarring St Clere.
- In Surrey: The manors of Burstow, Hedgecourt and Marden.
- In Kent: The manor of Wodeland. Woodland, alias Week, was a manor in the parish of West Kingsdown.
- In Buckinghamshire: The manor of Aston Chiverey in the parish of Aston Clinton.
- Northamptonshire: The manor of Old (alias Wold).

John was appointed Escheator (responsible for property seized by the king) of Northamptonshire and Rutland in 1446. John was one of six men appointed to enquire into various details of the manor of Geddington.

He was granted the post of Receiver of the Duchy of Lancaster and lands in Northamptonshire, Bedfordshire and Huntingdonshire.

He was born in 1420 at Surrey and died in 1475, aged 55.

ST CLERE

Lady Eleanor St Clere

Eleanor was the heiress to a substantial number of manors.

In 1445, the properties formerly held by Thomas St Clere, which had been taken into the King Henry IV's hands which were released. He was only a tenant.

She was born in 1425 at Sussex and died there at 1486, aged 61.

Sir Thomas St Clere married Margaret Hoo.

Children are <u>Eleanor</u>, two other daughters.

Thomas had no sons, but three daughters. They divided the extensive property between them.

He was born in 1401 and died in 1435, aged 34.

Sir Philip St Clere married Margaret de Loveyne of Burstow.

Children are John, <u>Thomas,</u> Margaret.

Philip served as High Sheriff of Surrey and Sussex in 1405.

A series of enquiries were held after Sir Philip's death to ascertain his property rights and the identity of his heir. These confirmed that Sir Philip had held properties in Cambridgeshire, Kent, Leicestershire, Oxfordshire, Somerset, Suffolk, Surrey and Sussex.

Philip's property ownership was as follows:

- In Somerset: The manor of Chiselborough.
- In Cambridgeshire: The manor of Swaffham Prior.
- In Suffolk: The manor of Withersfield.
- In Oxfordshire: The manors of Barton Steeple, Stanton St John and Chalgrove.
- In Surrey: The manors of Lagham (in the parish of Godstone), Marden, Hedgecourt and Burstow.
- In Sussex: The manors of Lavertye, Tarring Neville, Brambletye, Jevington, Heighton and Nutbourne.
- In Kent: The manor of West Aldham (in the parish of Ightham), the manor of Ospringe (near Faversham), Kemsing (part) and Woodland (in the parish of West Kingsdown); also, the reversion of Lullingstone Castle.
- In Leicestershire: The manor of Ashby Magna.

Sir Philip held the following property by the courtesy of England: The manors of Ensfield and Penshurst and other property at Ashour Park, Chiddingstone, Bidborough and Leigh.

He was born in 1362 and died in 1408 there at Penhurst, Sussex, aged 46.
She was born in 1372 and died in 1408 there at Godstone, Surrey, aged 36.

Sir Philip St Clere married Joan de Audley

Child is <u>Philip</u>.

He was born in 1330 at Sherburn, Oxfordshire and died in 1377 at Oxford, Oxfordshire, aged 47.

DE AUDLEY

Joan de Audley

She was born in 1300.

Sir James de Audley (or Audeley) of Wold

Children are James, Eva, Thomas, <u>Joan</u>.

James was one of the original knights, or founders, of the Order of the Garter. He served in Crecy, France, in 1346 with Edward the Black Prince.

He was born in 1318 and died in 1369, aged 51.

Hugh de Audley married Margaret de Clare at Windsor Castle in 1317.

Children are <u>James</u>, Margaret.

Hugh's titles included Baron Audley, Earl of Gloucestershire, Lord Chilton and Lord Gratton. He was Ambassador to France in 1341.

He was born in 1291 at Stratton Audley, Oxfordshire and died in 1347 at Tonbridge Priory, Kent, aged 56.

Hugh Audley the Elder married Isolde le Roue.

Child is <u>Hugh</u>.

Hugh was the first Baron of Gloucester. After rebelling with the Earl of Lancashire in 1322, he surrendered and was held in Wallington Castle.

He was born at 1267 at Stratton Audley, Oxfordshire and died in 1326, aged 59.
She died in 1294.

James de Audley married Countess Ela de Longespée.

Children are <u>Hugh</u>, James.

In 1257, James accompanied Richard, King of the Romans, to his coronation in Aachen, Paris, sailing on and returning to England in the autumn to take part in the Welsh campaign of 1257–1260.

In 1258 he was one of the royalist members of the council of fifteen nominated by the Provisions of Oxford and two years later he acted as an itinerant justice.

On Llewelyn of Wales attacking Mortimer, a royalist marcher, James joined Prince Edward at Hereford in 1263 to resist the invasion. However, the barons, coming to Llewelyn's assistance, dispersed the royalist forces and seized his castles and estates.

Early in 1265, James joined with other marchers to take part in the campaign of Evesham and the overthrow of the baronial party. He served as High Sheriff of Staffordshire and Shropshire in 1261 and 1270. During his tenure as Justiciar of Ireland he led several expeditions against the Irish rebels.

He was born in 1220 in Heleigh Castle, Staffordshire, and died in 1272 in Poiters, aged 52, by the Black Prince, who decided to honour his death.

LONGESPÉE

Countess Ela de Longespée

She was born in 1187 and died in 1261, aged 74.

Sir William Longespée I married Idione de Camville.

Children are <u>Ela</u>, William, Richard, Edmund.

William was an English knight and crusader. His death became of significant importance to the English psyche as he died at the Battle of Mansurah, near Al-Mansurah in Egypt.

In the first of William's two pilgrimages to the Holy Land he was a participant in the second wave of crusades, the Barons' Crusade. In 1240, he left England in the service of Richard, 1st Earl of Cornwall, with roughly a dozen English barons and several hundred knights. They made their way to Marseilles in mid-September, and landed at Acre. William almost certainly departed with Richard for England in 1241.

In the Seventh Crusade of 1247, William again made a pilgrimage to the Holy Land. He proceeded to Rome and made a plea to Pope Innocent IV for support. Having succeeded in gaining the favour of the Pope, William raised a company of 200 English horses to join King Louis on his crusade.

During the Seventh Crusade, William commanded the English forces. He became widely known for his feats of chivalry and his subsequent martyrdom. William and his men, along with 280 Knights Templar, were killed at this time.

He was born in 1212 and died in 1250 at St Cross in Acre in the Holy Land, aged 38
She was born in 1209 and died in 1251, aged 42.

Sir William Longespée II married Ela de Salisbury, 3rd Countess of Salisbury.

Child is <u>William</u>.

William was knighted 3rd Earl of Salisbury by his cousin Henry III in Gloucester in 1233, at Whitsuntide.

In 1230, as the wife of William, Countess Ela was instructed to surrender to him all the lands she held by her inheritance, along with other properties granted to her son by Henry in 1228.

William was to be closely associated with his royal cousin, largely in a military capacity. In 1233, during the rebellion of Richard Marshal, Earl of Pembroke, he was at Henry's side in the operations against the Welsh and other supporters of the Earl. In 1234 he was engaged in the pursuit and arrest of Peter des Rivaux.

William fought at the battle of Saintes in 1242 and was appointed captain of a number of subsequent operations, including the raid into Périgord in late 1242 and the siege of Garro in 1243. After returning to England, in 1245 William went in royal service to Wales.

He was born in 1176 and died in 1226, aged 50.
She was born in 1187 and died in 1261, aged 74.

Ida de Tosny, Countess of Norfolk

Henry Plantagenet had locked up his wife Eleanor of Aquitaine in 1173 for supporting their son's revolt against him. He was free to engage with Ida de Tosny whom he liked and was at his court. He had an illegitimate son named William.

Eleanor of Aquitaine was Queen Consort of France 1137–1152 and Duchess of Aquitaine in her own right. She was one of the wealthiest and most powerful women in Western Europe during the Middle Ages. She led several armies in her life and was a leader of the Second Crusade.

She (Ida) was born in 1156 and died in 1226, aged 70.

PLANTAGENET

Margaret de Clare, Countess of Gloucester, Countess of Cornwall.

She was an English Noblewoman, heiress, and the second-eldest of the three daughters of Gilbert de Clare, making her a grand-daughter of King Edward I of England.

However, Piers Gaveston her husband was executed only 6 months later leaving her a widow. She joined the royal family from London to York in 1316. Following the death of their brother, Gilbert de Clare, 7th Earl of Hertford, at the battle of Bannockburn in 1344, Margaret received a share of his inheritance. She was awarded the vast Gloucester estate and King Edward I arranged a second marriage for her to another favourite, Hugh de Audley,1st Earl of Gloucester at Windsor Castle.

She was born in 1293 at Tonbridge Castle, Kent and died in 1342 at Tonbridge Priory in Kent, aged 49.

Gilbert de Clare, 7th Earl of Gloucester married his second wife Princess Joan of Acre.

Children are <u>Margaret</u> and two other daughters.

He was also known as Red Gilbert de Clare or the Red Earl, probably because his hair colour or fiery temper in battle. He inherited all his father's estates in 1622.

During the Second Barons' War in 1264, Gilbert de Clare led the massacre of the Jews at Canterbury, as Simon de Montfort's supporters had done elsewhere. Gilbert de Clare's castles of Kingston and Tonbridge were taken by the King, Henry III.

In 1265, as a reward for supporting Prince Edward, Gilbert was given the castle and title of Abergavenny and honour and castle of Brecknock. At Michaelmas his disputes with Llewelyn the Last were submitted to arbitration, but without a final settlement. Meanwhile, he was building Caerphilly Castle into a fortress.

At the end of the year 1268 he refused to obey the King's summons to attend parliament, alleging that, owing to the constant inroads of Llewelyn the Last, his Welsh estates needed his presence for their defence. At the death of Henry III, 1272, the Earl took the lead in swearing fealty to Edward I, who was then in Sicily on his return from the Crusade.

During Edward's invasion of Wales in 1282, Clare insisted on leading an attack into southern Wales. King Edward made Clare the commander of the southern army invading Wales. However, Clare's army faced disaster after being heavily defeated at the Battle of Llandeilo Fawr. Following this defeat, Clare was relieved of his position as the southern commander.

In the next year, 1291, he quarrelled with the Earl of Hereford, Humphrey de Bohun, 3rd Earl of Hereford, grandson of his onetime guardian, about the Lordship of Brecknock, where Bohun accused Clare of building a castle on his land culminated in a private war between them. At this both were imprisoned by the King, both sentenced to having their lands forfeit for life and Clare, the Earl of Gloucester, as the aggressor, was fined 10,000 marks, and the Earl of Hereford 1,000 marks. They were released almost immediately and both of their lands completely restored to them.

He was born in 1243 at Christchurch Hampshire and died in 1295 at Monmouth Castle and buried in Tewkesbury Abbey, aged 52.

She was born in 1272.

Edward I, King of England married Eleanor of Castile Queen Consort of England.

Children are Edward 1307, <u>Joan of Acre</u> 1272

The first son of Henry III, Edward was involved from an early age in the political intrigues of his father's reign, which included an outright rebellion by the English barons. In 1259, he briefly sided with a baronial reform movement, supporting the Provisions of Oxford. After reconciliation with his father, however, he remained loyal throughout the subsequent armed conflict, known as the Second Barons' War After the Battle of Lewes, Edward was hostage to the rebellious barons, but escaped after a few months and defeated the baronial leader Simon de Montfort at the Battle of Evesham in 1265. Within two years the rebellion was extinguished and, with England pacified, Edward joined the Ninth Crusade to the Holy Land. He was on his way home in 1272 when he was informed that his father had died. Making a slow return, he reached England in 1274 and was crowned at Westminster Abbey.

Edward spent much of his reign reforming royal administration and common law. Through an extensive legal inquiry, he investigated the tenure of various feudal liberties, while the law was reformed through a series of statutes regulating criminal and property law. Increasingly, however, Edward's attention was drawn towards military affairs. After suppressing a minor rebellion in Wales in 1276–77, Edward responded to a second rebellion in 1282–83 with a full-scale war of conquest. After a successful campaign, he subjected Wales to English rule, built a series of castles and towns in the countryside and settled them with English people. Next, his efforts were directed towards the Kingdom of Scotland. Initially invited to arbitrate a succession dispute, Edward claimed feudal suzerainty over Scotland. The war that followed continued after Edward's death, even though the English seemed victorious at several points. Simultaneously, Edward found himself at war with France (a Scottish ally) after King Philip IV of France had confiscated the Duchy of Gascony, which until then had been held in personal union with the Kingdom of England. Although Edward recovered his duchy, this conflict relieved English military pressure against Scotland. At the same time there were problems at home. In the mid-1290s, extensive military campaigns required high levels of taxation, and Edward met with both lay and ecclesiastical opposition. These crises were initially averted, but issues remained unsettled. When the King died in 1307, he left to his son Edward II an ongoing war with Scotland and many financial and political problems.

Edward I was a tall man for his era, at 6 ft 2 in (1.88 m), hence the nickname "Longshanks". He was temperamental, and this, along with his height, made him an intimidating man, and he often instilled fear in his contemporaries. Nevertheless, he held the respect of his subjects for the way he embodied the medieval ideal of kingship, as a soldier, an administrator, and a man of faith. Modern historians are divided on their assessment of Edward: while some have praised him for his contribution to the law and administration, others have criticised him for his uncompromising attitude towards his nobility. Currently, Edward I is credited with many accomplishments during his reign, including restoring royal authority after the reign of Henry III, establishing Parliament as a permanent institution and thereby also a functional system for raising taxes, and reforming the law through statutes. At the same time, he is also often criticised for issuing the Edict of Expulsion in 1290, by which the Jews were expelled from England. The Edict remained in effect for the rest of the Middle Ages, and it was over 350 years until it was formally overturned under Oliver Cromwell in 1657.

He was born in 1272 and died in 1307 at Westminster Abbey, London, aged 35.
She was born in 1254 and died in 1280, aged 26.

Henry III, King of England married Eleanor of Provence at Canterbury Cathedral in 1236.

Children are Edward 1239, Margaret 1240, Beatrice 1242, Edmund 1245, Katherine 1253.

Henry III, also known as Henry of Winchester, was King of England, Lord of Ireland, and Duke of Aquitaine from 1216 until his death in 1272. The son of King John and Isabella of Angoulême, Henry assumed the throne when he was only nine in the middle of the First Barons' War. Cardinal Guala declared the war against the rebel barons to be a religious crusade and Henry's forces, led by William Marshal, defeated the rebels at the battles of Lincoln and Sandwich in 1217. Henry promised to abide by the Great Charter of 1225, a later version of the 1215 Magna Carta, which limited royal power and protected the rights of the major barons. His early rule was dominated first by Hubert de Burgh and then Peter des Roches, who re-established royal authority after the war. In 1230, the King attempted to reconquer the provinces of France that had once belonged to his father, but the invasion was a debacle. A revolt led by William Marshal's son, Richard Marshal, broke out in 1232, ending in a peace settlement negotiated by the Church.

Following the revolt, Henry ruled England personally, rather than governing through senior ministers. He travelled less than previous monarchs, investing heavily in a handful of his favourite palaces and castles. He married Eleanor of Provence, with whom he had five children. Henry was known for his piety, holding lavish religious ceremonies and giving generously to charities; the King was particularly devoted to the figure of Edward the Confessor, whom he adopted as his patron saint. He extracted huge sums of money from the Jews in England, ultimately crippling their ability to do business, and as attitudes towards the Jews hardened, he introduced the Statute of Jewry, attempting to segregate the community. In a fresh attempt to reclaim his family's lands in France, he invaded Poitou in 1242, leading to the disastrous Battle of Taillebourg. After this, Henry relied on diplomacy, cultivating an alliance with Frederick II, Holy Roman Emperor. Henry supported his brother Richard of Cornwall in his bid to become King of the Romans in 1256, but was unable to place his own son Edmund Crouchback on the throne of Sicily, despite investing large amounts of money. He planned to go on crusade to the Levant, but was prevented from doing so by rebellions in Gascony.

By 1258, Henry's rule was increasingly unpopular, the result of the failure of his expensive foreign policies and the notoriety of his Poitevin half-brothers, the Lusignans, as well as the role of his local officials in collecting taxes and debts. A coalition of his barons, initially probably backed by Eleanor, seized power in a coup d'état and expelled the Poitevins from England, reforming the royal government through a process called the Provisions of Oxford. Henry and the baronial government enacted a peace with France in 1259, under which Henry gave up his rights to his other lands in France in return for King Louis IX recognising him as the rightful ruler of Gascony. The baronial regime collapsed but Henry was unable to reform a stable government and instability across England continued.

In 1263, one of the more radical barons, Simon de Montfort, seized power, resulting in the Second Barons' War. Henry persuaded Louis to support his cause and mobilised an army. The Battle of Lewes occurred in 1264, where Henry was defeated and taken prisoner. Henry's eldest son, Edward, escaped from captivity to defeat de Montfort at the Battle of Evesham the following year and freed his father. Henry initially enacted a harsh revenge on the remaining rebels, but was persuaded by the Church to mollify his policies through the Dictum of Kenilworth. Reconstruction was slow and Henry had to acquiesce to various measures, including further suppression of the Jews, to maintain baronial and popular support. Henry died in 1272, leaving Edward as his successor. He was buried in Westminster Abbey, which he had rebuilt in the second half of his reign, and was moved to his current tomb in 1290. Some miracles were declared after his death; however, he was not canonised. Henry's reign of fifty-six years was the longest in medieval English history and would not be surpassed by an English, or later British, monarch until that of George III in the nineteenth century.

He was born in 1207 and died in 1272, aged 65.
She was born in 1224 and died in 1257, aged 33.

John, King of England married his first wife Isabelle de Clere, Countess of Gloucester.

She remained in prison and was released in 1214. He married his second wife Isabella of Angoulême in 1200.

Children are <u>Henry</u> 1207, Richard 1209, Joan 1210, Isabella 1214, Eleanor 1215.

John was King of England from 1199 until his death in 1216. He lost the Duchy of Normandy and most of his other French lands to King Philip II of France, resulting in the collapse of the Angevin Empire and contributing to the subsequent growth in power of the French Capetian dynasty during the 13th century. The baronial revolt at the end of John's reign led to the sealing of Magna Carta, a document sometimes considered an early step in the evolution of the constitution of the United Kingdom.

John was the youngest of the four surviving sons of King Henry II of England and Duchess Eleanor of Aquitaine. He was nicknamed John Lackland because he was not expected to inherit significant lands He became Henry's favourite child following the failed revolt of 1173–1174 by his brothers Henry the Young King, Richard, and Geoffrey against the King. John was appointed the Lord of Ireland in 1177 and given lands in England and on the continent. John unsuccessfully attempted a rebellion against the royal administrators of his brother, King Richard, whilst Richard was participating in the Third Crusade, but he was proclaimed king after Richard died in 1199. He came to an agreement with Philip II of France to recognise John's possession of the continental Angevin lands at the peace treaty of Le Goulet in 1200.

When war with France broke out again in 1202, John achieved early victories, but shortages of military resources and his treatment of Norman, Breton, and Anjou nobles resulted in the collapse of his empire in northern France in 1204. He spent much of the next decade attempting to regain these lands, raising huge revenues, reforming his armed forces and rebuilding continental alliances. His judicial reforms had a lasting effect on the English common law system, as well as providing an additional source of revenue. An argument with Pope Innocent III led to John's excommunication in 1209, a dispute he finally settled in 1213. John's attempt to defeat Philip in 1214 failed because of the French victory over John's allies at the battle of Bouvines. When he returned to England, John faced a rebellion by many of his barons, who were unhappy with his fiscal policies and his treatment of many of England's most powerful nobles. Although both John and the barons agreed to the Magna Carta peace treaty in 1215, neither side complied with its conditions. Civil war broke out shortly afterwards, with the barons aided by Louis VIII of France. It soon descended into a stalemate. John died of dysentery contracted whilst on campaign in eastern England during late 1216; supporters of his son Henry III went on to achieve victory over Louis and the rebel barons the following year.

He was born in 1167 at Beaumont palace, Oxfordshire and died in 1216 at Newark Castle, Nottinghamshire, aged 49.
She was born in 1189.

FRANKISH EMPIRE

King Henry II had an illegitimate son by Ide Tosny, Countess of Norfolk.

Children are Richard, Geoffrey, <u>John</u>. Illegitimate are Geoffrey, <u>William</u>.

Henry was King of England from 1154 until his death. He was the first king of the House of Plantagenet. King Louis VII of France made him Duke of Normandy in 1150. Henry became Count of Anjou and Maine upon the death of his father, Count Geoffrey V, in 1151.

In 1152, Henry married Eleanor of Aquitaine, whose marriage to Louis VII had recently been annulled; this made him Duke of Aquitaine. He became Count of Nantes by treaty in 1185.

Before he was 40, he controlled England, large parts of Wales, the eastern half of Ireland and the western half of France, an area that would later come to be called the Angevin Empire. At various times, Henry also partially controlled Scotland, Wales and the Duchy of Brittany.

Henry was an energetic and sometimes ruthless ruler, driven by a desire to restore the lands and privileges of his grandfather, Henry I. During the early years of his reign, the younger Henry restored the royal administration in England, re-established ownership over Wales and gained full control over his lands in Anjou, Maine and Touraine.

Henry's desire to reform the relationship between the Church and Crown led to conflict with his former friend Thomas Becket, the Archbishop of Canterbury. This controversy lasted for much of the 1160s and resulted in Becket's murder in 1170.

Henry soon came into conflict with Louis VII, and the two rulers fought what has been termed a 'cold war' over several decades. Henry expanded his empire at Louis's expense, taking Brittany and pushing east into central France and south into Toulouse; despite numerous peace conferences and treaties, no lasting agreement was reached.

As the sons of the two kings grew up (Henry and Louis), tensions over the future inheritance of the empire began to emerge. The Great Revolt was only defeated by Henry's vigorous military action and talented local commanders, many of them new men appointed for their loyalty and administrative skills.

Henry was a driving force in the creation of a genuinely English monarchy and, ultimately, a unified Britain. During the Victorian expansion of the British Empire, historians were keenly interested in the formation of Henry's own empire, but they also expressed concern over his private life and treatment of Becket.

He was born in 1133 and died in 1189, aged 56.

Geoffrey V married Empress Matilda in 1128.

Children are <u>Henry</u>, Geoffrey, William, Emma.

Geoffrey – called the Handsome, the Fair (in French 'le Bel') or Plantagenet – was, from 1129, the Count of Anjou, Touraine and Maine by inheritance, and also, from 1144, the Duke of Normandy by conquest. His marriage to Empress Matilda, daughter of King Henry I of England, led to the centuries-long reign of the Plantagenet dynasty in England.

Geoffrey received his nickname from the yellow sprig of broom blossom that he wore in his hat. He was handsome, red haired, jovial and a great warrior. King Henry I of England, having heard reports of Geoffrey's talents and prowess, sent legates to Anjou to negotiate a marriage between his 25-year-old daughter Matilda and Geoffrey.

The marriage was meant to seal a lasting peace between England, Normandy (an English possession since William I) and Anjou. Matilda was 11 years older than Geoffrey and very proud of her status as Dowager Empress (as opposed to being a mere Countess), which she kept for the remainder of her life. The marriage was a stormy but happy one, with frequent long separations.

The year after the marriage, Geoffrey's father left for Jerusalem (where he was later to become king), leaving Geoffrey behind as Count of Anjou. Geoffrey secured all of Normandy west and south of the Seine, crossed the Seine and entered Rouen. He assumed the title Duke of Normandy in the summer of 1144 and founded an Augustine priory at Château-l'Hermitage in Anjou.

Henry II took his father's place as head of the Plantagenet ducal house. In 1153, the Treaty of Wallingford stipulated that Stephen should remain King of England for life and that Henry II, the son of Geoffrey and Matilda, should succeed him, beginning the Plantagenet era in English history.

He was born in 1113 and died in 1151 at St Julien's Cathedral in Le Mans, France, aged 38.

Fulk, King of Jerusalem, married Eremburge de Beaugency.

Children are <u>Geoffrey V</u>, Sibylla, Matilda.

Fulk (in Latin, 'Fulco', in French, 'Foulque' or 'Foulques'), also known as Fulk the Younger, was Count of Anjou, and the King of Jerusalem from 1131 until his death.

He was originally an opponent of King Henry I of England and a supporter of King Louis VI of France. However, in 1118 or 1119, he made an alliance with Henry when he arranged for his daughter Matilda to marry Henry's son William Adelin.

Fulk went on crusade in 1119 or 1120 and became attached to the Knights Templar (Orderic Vitalis). He returned late in 1121, after which he began to subsidise the Templars, maintaining two knights in the Holy Land for a year.

Fulk was a wealthy crusader and experienced military commander. His experience in the field would prove invaluable. His chief fault was an inability to remember names and faces.

Jerusalem's northern border was of great concern. Fulk had been appointed Regent of the Principality of Antioch and strengthened the kingdom's southern border. The city was a base from which the Egyptian Fatimids launched frequent raids on the Kingdom of Jerusalem and Fulk sought to neutralise this threat.

He was born in 1089 at Angers and died in 1143 at Acre, Jerusalem, aged 54.

Fulk IV married Bertrade de Mounford in 1089.

Children are Emengarde, Geoffrey IV, <u>Fulk</u>.

Fulk (in French, Foulques IV), called le Réchin, was Count of Anjou. He was noted to be a man with many uncontrollable habits.

Much of Fulk's rule was devoted to regaining control over the Angevin Baronage and to a complex struggle with Normandy for influence in Maine and Brittany.

He may have married as many as five times; there is some doubt regarding the exact number of his wives and how many he repudiated or disowned.

He was born in 1043 and died in 1109, aged 66.

Geoffrey II married Emengard of Anjou, Duchess of Burgundy, in 1035.

Children are Hildegarde, Geoffrey III, <u>Fulk IV</u>.

Geoffrey de Château-Landon was the Count of Gâtinais. He was the son of Hugues du Perche, Count of Gâtinais, and his mother was Béatrice de Mâcon, the daughter of Aubry II de Mâcon.

Geoffrey married the Duchess of Burgundy, daughter of Fulk III, Count of Anjou. After Geoffrey's death his widow married Robert I, Duke of Burgundy.

He was born in 1000 and died in 1046, aged 46.

Hugues du Perche married Béatrice de Mâcon.

Children are <u>Geoffrey II</u>, Liétaud.

Hugues was a tenth-century French nobleman. He was the youngest son of Fulcois, Count of Perche, probably of the family of viscounts from Châteaudun.

He married Béatrice, the widow of Geoffroy I, Count of Gatinais, and thus became Count of Gâtinais, a leading French nobleman.

Châteaudun is closely associated with the County of Perche, and the early rulers generally held titles of both Viscount of Châteaudun and Count of Perche. There are also close ties between these counts and the counts of Anjou, and members of the House of Ingelger and the House of Plantagenet descended from this line.

He died in 1031.

Fulcuich du Perche married Melissant de Chateaudun.

He was born in 950 and died in 1023, aged 73.
She was born in 955 and died in 1040, aged 85.

Geoffery I married Hildegarde du Perche.

Geoffery was Viscount of Chartres and Count of Chateaudun.

He was born in 920 and died in 985, aged 65.

Vicomte Geoffroi de Chartres married Emengarde.

Children are <u>Goeffroy</u>, Gilduin, Isobeau, Geoffroi.

He was born in 890 and died in 942, aged 52.

SECTION 5: A TIMELINES

Wyeth

Robert Malcolm Wyeth	1952		Still living
Malcolm George R Wyeth	1919–2003	m	**Dorothy Fisher in 1949**
George William Wyeth	1875–1955	m	Margurrite King in 1917
George Champness Wyeth	1848–1927	m	**Martha French in 1869**
William Henry Wyeth	1810–1871	m	Millicent Wyeth in 1837
William Wyeth	1783–1843	m	Martha Selway in 1804
Charles Wyath	1744–1831	m	Sarah Rampton in 1773
Abraham Wyeth	1721–1781	m	Elizabeth Humber in 1737
George Wythe	1680–1740	m	Barbara Nash in 1718
Thomas Withe	1620–1690	m	Mary Wythe
Richard Wythe		m	Joane Wythe
John Wythe	1561–1605	m	Emma Elizabeth Jannings in 1573
Thomas Wythe	1532–1593	m	Alice de Girling in 1559
John Wythe	1505–1544	m	Margaret Willington in 1531
Oliver Wyse	1465–1505	m	Margaret Elizabeth Tremayne

Fisher

Dorothy Fisher	1918–2012		
Frederick Charles Fisher	1892–1972	m	**Lucretia Wyard in 1918**
James John Fisher	1845–1894	m	**Emily Isobella Comport in 1880**
Matthew Fisher	1814–1859	m	Mary Hardingham in 1820
John Fisher	1760–1853	m	Jane Parratt in 1785
Matthew Fisher	1736–1814	m	Susanna Rushton in 1760
John Fisher	1699–1748	m	Mary Wright in 1726
William Fisher	1672–1750	m	Elizabeth Bean in 1698
Christopher Fisher	1641	m	Elizabeth Williams

Comport

Emily Isabella Comport	1854–1946		
Charles Comport	1820–1888	m	Mary Ann Roper in 1840
Ebenezer Comport	1784–1856	m	Elizabeth
Joseph Comport	1737–1808	m	Susanna French in 1776
Ebenezar Comport	1704–1765	m	Elizabeth Steely in 1728
Ebenezer Comport	1675–1733	m	Mary Stephens in 1697
Nicholas Comport	1679	m	?

Wyard

Lucretia Dolly Wyard	1896–1996		
Ephraim Wyard	1839–1904	m	Susan Caddy in 1891
Walter Wyard	1808–1848	m	Susan Cadman in 1836
William Wyard	1780	m	Frances Harnton
Thomas Wyard	1743–1811	m	Ann Maxim in 1777
William Wyard	1706–1781	m	Elizabeth Bruer in 1737
William Wyard	1667–1746	m	Ann Westham in 1699
William Wyard	1630–1694	m	Hannah Cooper in 1664
James Wyard	1608–1653	m	Elizabeth Covell in 1621
William Wyard	1557–1630	m	Elizabeth James
Humfrey Wyard	1530–1597	m	Elizabeth Facebrown in 1563
Richard Wyard	1478–1560	m	Agnes Hawes in 1523
Randall Wyard		m	Ann Wyard

Spink to Pipe

Carol Spink	1957		Still living
Eric Douglas Spink	1927–2107	m	**Kathleen Irene M. Rutter in 1953**
Frederick William Spink	1894–1960	m	**Ethel Maud Perry in 1921**
James William Spink	1849–1960	m	Elizabeth Rivers in 1883
William Spink	1817–1902	m	Mary Ann Rivers in 1842
Issac Spink	1781–1850	m	Ann Pipe in 1803

William Pipe	1750–1827	m	Hannah Greenard in 1774
Edward Pipe	1715–1827	m	Elizabeth Stannard in 1746
John Pipe	1674–1720	m	Mary Ralf in 1709
William Pipe	1649–1731	m	Anne Girling in 1670
Wylam Pipe	1611–1650	m	Sarah Neal in 1634
William Pipe	1586–1622	m	Rebecca Rebacker in 1611
Jerome Pipe	1563–1631	m	Margaret Dowsing in 1585
William Pipe (the elder)	1530–1580	m	Mildred Thymblethorpe in 1550
Thomas Pipe	1500–1560	m	Margaret in 1517
William Pipe	1485–1517	m	Margery

Perry, Poole to Westwood

Ethel Maud Perry	1897–1975		
Henry Percy Perry	1874–1942	m	Alice Jane Baker in 1895
George Perry	1833–1915	m	Sarah Elizabeth Poole in 1857
William Poole	1809–1892	m	Margaret Harris in 1838
Edward Poole	1767–1838	m	Hannah Bright in 1792
Edward Poole	1739–1832	m	Elizabeth Westwood in 1761
William John Westwood	1699–1767	m	Ann Luck in 1724
Thomas William Westwood	1668–1725	m	Elizabeth Beverley in 1693
Thomas Westwood	1645–1691	m	Hannah Lewis in 1665
Henry Westwood Yeoman	1619–1683	m	Mary Butcher in 1645
Nicholas Westwood	1590–1678	m	Katherine Morgan in 1609
Nicholas Westwood	1565	m	Grace Turnish in 1591
Nicholas Westwood	1510	m	?

Rutter

| Kathleen Irene Maud Rutte | 1931 | | Still living |
| Percy Pearson G Rutter | 1906–1995 | m | **Mary Maud Adelaide Blunt in 1927** |

Frank Rutter	1872–1949	m	Florence Louise Clarke in 1897
William Rutter	1828–1904	m	Lucy Moore in 1872
Joseph Rutter	1790–1861	m	Mary Ann Haygreen in 1822
Joseph Rutter	1753–1824	m	Prudence Hurrell in 1783
Thomas Rutter	1713–1778	m	Sarah Richardson
John Rutterforth Rutter	1680–1765	m	Susannah Boarly
Thomas Rutter	1647–1702	m	Ann in 1681
Thomas Rutterforth	1699	m	Anne Rutherforth in 1645
William Rutterforth	1567–1653	m	?
William Rutter		m	?

Blunt

Mary Maud Adelaide Blunt	1903–1976		
William Blunt	1864	m	Sarah Peacock in 1890
Daniel Blunt	1838–1908	m	Johanna Ashman in 1862
William Blunt	1812–1891	m	Eliza Hanslow in 1834
Thomas Blunt	1793–1868	m	Esther Danks in 1812
William Blunt	1755–1796	m	Prudence Jesson in 1774
George Blunt	1739–1763	m	Mary Edwards in 1749
George Blunt	1692	m	Ann Reane in 1706
George Blunt	1678	m	Ann Clarke in 1692
Thomas Blunt	1630–1684	m	?

French, Elliot, Burfield to Forde

Martha French	1847–1917		
William French	1816–1896	m	Harriet Flexman in 1842
George French	1779–1867	m	Jenny Elliot
Thomas Elliot	1744–1808	m	Sarah Burfield in 1777
William Burfield	1715–1760	m	Ann Bridger in 1740
John Burfield	1686–1754	m	Elizabeth Ellis in 1714
Robert Burfield	1660–1725	m	Mary Streeter in 1667
Abraham Burfield	1615–1684	m	Sybil Hale in 1641

Abraham Burfield	1590–1637	m	Juditha Ford in 1610
Richarde Forde	1540–1596	m	Ann Tyler in 1578
Richard Forde	1530–1604	m	Katherine Hide in 1544
John Aford	1505–1545	m	Lady Alice Gage in 1524

Gage, St Clere, de Audley to Longespée

Sir John Gage KG	1479–1556	m	Philippa de Guildeford in 1501
William Gage	1450–1496	m	Agnes Bolney
Sir John Gage	1420–1475	m	Lady Eleanor St Clere
Sir Thomas St Clere	1401–1435	m	Margaret Hoo
Sir Philip St Clere	1362–1408	m	Margaret de Loveyne of Burstow
Sir Philip St Clere	1330–1377	m	?
Sir James de Audley of Wold	1318–1369	m	Joan de Audley
Hugh de Audley	1291–1347	m	**Margaret de Clare in 1317**
Hugh Audley Elder	1226–1326	m	Isolde le Roue
James de Audley	1220–1272	m	**Countess Ela de Longespée**
Sir William Longespée I	1212–1250	m	Idone de Camville
Sir William Longespée II	1176–1226	m	3rd Countess Ela de Salisbury

Plantagenet

Margaret de Clare			
Gilbert de Clare	1243–1295	m	Princess Joan of Acre
King Edward I	1272–1307	m	Eleanor of Castile
King Henry III	1207-1272	m	Eleanor of Provence in 1236
King John	1167-1216	m	Isabelle de Clere

Frankish Empire

King Henry II	1133–1189	m	Eleanor of Aquitaine, 1152
		i	Ide Tosny, Countess of Norfolk
Geoffrey V	1113–1151	m	Empress Matilda in 1128

Fulk, King of Jerusalem	1089–1109	m	Eremburge de Beaugency
Fulk IV	1034–1109	m	Bertrade de Mounford in 1089
Geoffrey II	1000–1046	m	Emengard of Anjou in 1035
Hugues du Perche	1031	m	Béatrice de Mâcon
Fulcuich du Perche	950–1023	m	Melissant de Chateaudun
Geoffrey I	920–985	m	Hildegrade du Perche
Geoffroi de Chartres	890–942	m	Emengarde

Lightning Source UK Ltd.
Milton Keynes UK
UKHW041559060722
405441UK00012B/264